John James Wilkinson

Receipts and Expenses in the Building of Bodmin Church

A.D. 1469 to 1472

John James Wilkinson

Receipts and Expenses in the Building of Bodmin Church
A.D. 1469 to 1472

ISBN/EAN: 9783337162290

Printed in Europe, USA, Canada, Australia, Japan

Cover: Foto ©ninafisch / pixelio.de

More available books at **www.hansebooks.com**

RECEIPTS AND EXPENSES

IN THE

BUILDING OF BODMIN CHURCH,

A.D. 1469 TO 1472.

EDITED BY THE

REV. JOHN JAMES WILKINSON, M.A.

RECTOR OF LANTEGLOS AND ADVENT.

PRINTED FOR THE CAMDEN SOCIETY.

M.DCCC.LXXIV.

PREFACE.

THE following account of the receipts and expenses in the rebuilding of the parish church of Bodmin was accidentally discovered in an old chest, in the parvise over the church-porch, early in the present century. It is neatly written in a book now severed into loose sheets, which, although preserved with great care, is becoming rapidly reduced to dust. There are discrepancies in the sums of the items, owing probably to the defective state of the manuscript. With the exception of the extension of the contractions, in italics, the whole is given as it was found, without any attempt at correction.

The rebuilding commenced in 1469 and was completed in 1472. There is scarcely a parish in Cornwall which does not bear testimony to the energy displayed in church restoration at that period. In many instances we find a south aisle rebuilt or added, in which, if the original church was cruciform, the south transept was absorbed. At the time when church restoration made such progress the nation was in a state of turmoil from the rival claims of Henry VI. and Edward IV. The isolated position of the county probably enabled the inhabitants to turn their attention to more peaceful pursuits, for history is silent as to any part taken in the strife by the county of Cornwall.

Of Bodmin Church the west end, tower, north chancel, aisle, and chancel were not rebuilt. The west door * was a fine specimen of Norman architecture. The tower, surmounted by a spire which was destroyed by lightning in 1699, had probably been erected in the previous century.

There is a payment for " possyng," *i.e.* propping up, " the rof of the chanseler " while the arches which separate it from the aisles were being erected. As the patrons, the prior and convent of the adjoining monastery of St. Petrock, did not in any way contribute to the rebuilding of the rest of the church, they defrayed the expense connected with the repair of the chancel, if anything was done to it. The seating and pulpit were not commenced till 1491, when a contract was signed for their completion by Michaelmas, 1495, at a cost of 92*l.*, the parish providing the wainscot timber.

The accounts commence with the receipts and expenses during the years 1469 and 1470, until Michaelmas 1471, while Thomas Jerman was receiver, and are summed up as follows:

	£	s.	d.
Receipts .	196	7	4½
Expenses	194	3	6½

In the following year Thomas Lucomb, then mayor, was receiver:

	£	s.	d.
Receipts .	65	7	0
Expenses	74	14	3

The whole sum expended was 268*l.* 17*s.* 9½*d.*; in addition to which, windows, trees, and other materials and labour were contributed.

Irrespective of the information obtained directly from these Accounts as to the means used for obtaining the necessary funds for the re-edification of the church, and the cost of labour towards the end of the fifteenth century, they are of great interest from

* For a full account of the church see Sir John Maclean's History of Trigg Minor, in which there is a drawing of this doorway.

the light which they throw on the social condition of the town of Bodmin at that period, and there is no reason to believe that Bodmin formed an exception to the general state of society in other towns at the same date. They exhibit a remarkable unanimity in the good work. Everyone seems to have given according to his means, and up to his means. Many who gave money gave labour also, many who could nót give money laboured as best they might, and others gave what they could. We have gifts of lambs, of a cow, and of a goose; and one woman in addition to her subscription sold her crokke for 20d.; and all found its way into the common treasury. No age or sex seems to have kept aloof. We find a "hold woman" contributing 3s. 2½d.; while the maidens in Fore Street and Bore Street gave subscriptions, in addition to the sums received from the Gilds of Virgins in the same streets. The Vicar gave his year's salary, and the "parish pepell," who lived out of the town, contributed 19s.

Much of the zeal shown may, we think, be attributed to the influence exercised by the Gilds. It is only recently we have become acquainted, and even now only partially so, with the degree in which religious life permeated society in the middle ages, particularly in the fifteenth century, through the minor confraternities. In Bodmin, at the period in question, almost the whole population seems to have been included in one or other of the Gilds, and it was through the means of their zeal and organization that the money required for rebuilding the Church was obtained without much difficulty. In the first place the Gilds contributed very freely from their own funds. We have seen that during the first three years of the work the total receipts from all sources amounted to 196l. 7s. 4d.; of which amount the Gilds contributed in money

86l. 11s. 5d. and *24l. 13s.* part of a collection by the Trades Gilds
of a penny per man of some, and a halfpenny of others, " the pore
comenys," throughout the town.   In addition to this they gave
wax to the value of *4l. 13s. 4d.*   The remainder of the sum was
made up of *50l. 8s.*, being a voluntary contribution of the inhabitants
generally, a bequest of *6l. 13s. 4d.*, the proceeds of the sale of old
materials, and from other miscellaneous sources.   In the following
year the Gilds were not less active and liberal.

Of these fraternities the Accounts disclose the names of upwards
of 40.   Five of these were Trades Gilds, or Gilds founded for the
interests of certain crafts.   These were St. Petroc (Skinners and
Glovers), SS. Dunstan and Eloy (Smiths), St. Anian the Bishop
(Cordenerys, Cordwainers), St. Martin the Bishop (Milwardys,
Millers or Millwrights), and St. John the Baptist, of whom no trade
is named, but probably the Gild consisted of Tailors and Drapers.
All the others were established for social and religious objects, for
the glory of God and the good of man.

Judging from the price of labour, the value of money was about
eight times greater than it is now.   A mason and stone-cutter
received *6d.* a day, a helyer or slater *5d.*, a plasterer *5½d.*, and a
common labourer and quarryman *3d.*

Annexed to the Accounts are the names of 460 inhabitants of
the town, who voluntarily subscribed to the rebuilding of the
church.   Many of these names are extinct or merged into other
families, but there are still some representatives of those who thus
substantially showed their veneration for the house of God, who are
at present about to tread in their steps by endeavouring to restore to
its former beauty the holy place around which sleep their honoured
remains.

The Editor begs to express his gratitude to the late Mr. Richard Bray, the Town Clerk of Bodmin, for having granted, often at inconvenience to himself, access to the documents of the Corporation, and to his son, Mr. George Bray, Sir John Maclean, and the Rev. William Iago, for their valuable assistance in deciphering their tattered remains.

In conclusion, he dedicates this attempt to elucidate the History of Bodmin to Commander James Liddell, R.N. J.P. and Alderman of the Borough of Bodmin, in remembrance of a friendship extending over nearly a quarter of a century.

Hic liber dico constat ecclesie pertinentia ad Eccle-
siam Parochialem Bodminie videlicet compotus
Thome Jerman pro fabrica Ecclesie.

Remembrans of all the Reseytis as for the byllynge of
the Parish Church of Bodmyn, fro the feste . . . . . .
Domini 1469° vnto Mychelmas Anno Domini * 1470ᵐᵒ,
& Anno Domini 1471°.

Inprimis, of Thomas Carter for a holde cofer of the Church recevyd	vj d.
Item of Joh.	
Item de Will. Androwe for olde tymber and moris †	xj d.
Item the same of	xviij d.
Item of Isbell lynche for olde tymber . . .	iiij d.
Item of John Proute for a lytell sta	viij d.
Item of John Cok for old tymber	iiij d.
Item of Thomas Dawne for a holde cofer . .	viij d.
Item of Will. Androwe for stonys of the Church .	ij s. vj d.
Item of mony fonde yn the church, that is to sey of Thomas Lucombe,‡ Robert Dyer, Bartholomew Trote, and Thomas Wylliam	v d.

* Henry Gurlyn was vicar, but he died shortly after the commencement of the work. Shields bearing his arms, some of them unfinished, are on the roof-bosses in the nave.

† "Mores," a word still in common use in Cornwall for the roots of trees.

‡ Roof-bosses display shields of Lucombe arms. Barth. Trote's merchant's mark is carved on bench-ends.

Item of Thomas Barbor, and feliship* for olde tymber   xl d.

Item for iij. copelles † of Thomas   .   .   .   .

Item of John Burnarde for a copelle   .   .   .   viij d.

Item of John Roby for a copelle   .   .   .   .   viij d.

Item of . . . . for a cage that the smale bell range yn   j d.

Item for iiij. copelles of Bartholomew Trote   .   .   ij s. viij d.

Item of Thomas Jerman for a holde copelle   .   .   viij d.

Item of John Philyp for a holde tre   .   .   .   x d.

Item of Bartholomew Trote for stonys y solde at quary   vj s. viij d.

Item of John Rawe for old lathis of the church   .   ij d.

Item of Robert Best for a holde copell   .   .   .   viij d.

Item the dutis siny . . . . . for stonys sold   .   .   xij d.

Item y recevyd of Harre Sturgen yeft ‡ mony   .   .   iiij d.

Item of Thomas Hancok .   .   .   .   .   .   ij d.

Item ther was sold to Sir § William the Parish Preste
for olde tymber, the vayle ‖   .   .   .   .   ij s. iiij d.

Item recevyd for a wyndowe y sold to the Parish of
Hellond .   .   .   .   xxvj s.

Item y recevyd for a wyndowe ¶ of Seynt Kewa   xxvj s. viij d.

Summa iiij li. ij s. j d.

Also y haue recevyd of the churche wexe perteynynge
to the Ildis ** y . . . . . vj^{li} at x^c .   .   .   . . . iij d.

Item y recevyd of men at quary dyuers tymys   .   .   ij s.

---

* "feleship," company.

† Couple-close, a pair of spars for a roof.

‡ gift-money.

§ "Sir," a common title of the clergy, as Shakespeare's Sir Hugh Evans. William
Bray was instituted on the death of Gurlyng, March 28, 1470. See Maclean's Trigg
Minor, p. 147.

‖ value.

¶ Many remains of a window containing incidents in our Lord's life are still in
the east window in the north aisle at St. Kew, and said by tradition to have belonged
originally to Bodmin.

** A contribution from the Gilds (ildis) of wax for the Church.

Item y recevyd of William Glynn fro a hold woman
yn the Reynstret . . . . . . iij s. ij d ob.

Item for the barris * y sold yn Lestithiell stret recevyd   xij d.

Item for the barris y . . . . . .

Item recevyd of Stephen Greby of mony left fetchynge
the organys fro Exeter . . . . .   ij s.

Item recevyd for a cowe that Raf Miller yeff† to the
work . . . . vij s. vj d.

Item y recevyd for a pot y sold that John Nordon yef   iij s. vij d.

Item y recevyd ‡ of dyuers men of the towne that
fayled here jornayes at quary, ffrust . . . John
  iiij d.   iiij d.   iiij d.
Bowyer, Robert Cok, William Reue, Thomas
  iiij d.   iiij d.   iiij d.   iiij d.
Archer, John Cok, Andrew Opy, John Watte,
  ij d.
William Dreyn, Ric. . . . . at more,
  iiij d.   iiij d.   iiij d.
William Pole, John Trefarthian, Thomas Crispyn,
  iiij d.   iiij d.   iiij d.
Raf Credy, Jeruys Teyler, John Salisbery, John
  iiij d.
Nytherton.

              Summa iiij li. xviij s.

Also y recevyd of Sir John Yeme for parte of a bequest of Isbell ffuller . . . . xxvj s. viij d.

Item of William Mason of parte of arrerages § of ac-
compt of the wardeship by the honds of Thomas
Lucombe . . . .   x s.

Item recevyd of Margaret, suster of Thomas Bere .   x s.

Item of John Wylle of Granpound . . . .   v s.

---

* Probably the old iron from the windows.   † gave.
‡ These receipts were probably fines.
§ arrears. "He'll grant the tribute, send the *arrearages*." Cymbeline, Act. ii.
Scene 4.

Item of Thomas Luchy	xl d.
Item of Shirston	iij s. iv d.
Item of Thomas Trote	x s.
. . . . . . Thomas Bere for a jorney to fetch lyme .	
Item of a man of Exeter	iiij d.
Item of a prest	j d.
Item of a . . . person	xx d.
Item of Thomas Watte for a plank y sold . .	vij d.
Item of Hancok Harry	x s.
Item of the . . . . of John Netherton . . .	ij s.
Item of Thomas Colom	ij d.
Item of John Togyon for a hold chandeler sold .	ij s.
Item of Edmond Beket for old lathis sold . .	xx d.
Item of Thomas Lucombe for old tymber . .	xij d.
Item off . . . . . Jerman for old tymber . . .	iij d.
Item to Bartholomew Trote for crestis,* iij. pipis, bordis, and old twistis †	v d.
Item the seide Bartholomew for old gare ‡ . .	vj d.

Summa iiij li. xij s. viij d.

Memorandum that Thomas for seide hath recevyd of the stewardis of the Ridyng § Ildis as for holdyng of . . . . by . . . . of ston made and ratid.

---

* " Crest " and " crecis," tiles to cover the ridge of the roof.
† Hinges are still sometimes called *twists.*
‡ gear, stuff.
§ Ildis, Guild or Gild. The festival of the " Ryding Gilds," held on the Sunday and Monday after the feast of St. Thomas the Martyr (Becket), July 7th, is thought by some to have been established in commemoration of the recovery of St. Petrock's bones in 1177; by others to have been a continuation of the old Floralia.

Having elected a " steward," the trading gilds, masters and apprentices, bearing the emblems of their trades, with the town's folk generally, attended church on the Sunday, and on their return distributed the church-ale from house to house, receiving from the inhabitants contributions according to their means. On the following day the gilds went in procession on horseback (whence the name) to the Priory, where they received " garlands gay." After this the sports began, and the revelry became

ffrust for seynt Loy is Ilde of John Hancok . xiij s. iiij d.
Item of seynt Petrok is Ilde of Richard Colom . xiij s. iiij d.
Item of seynt John is Ilde of John Prowte . xxvj s. viij d.
Item of seynt Anyan is Ilde of Thomas Hay . xxvj s. viij d.
Item of seynt Martyn is Ilde of Thomas ffykk . xiij s. iiij d.
Summa iiij li. xiij s. iiij d.

Memorandum of the receipt off the Ildis longyng to
the Church and Parish that the seide Thomas
recevyd.
ffrust off Erasmos Episcopi is Ilde . . . x li. ij s. xj d.
Item de gilda Beate Marie virginis in capella Sancti
Georgii Martyris . . . . . . xx s.
Item de gilda Beate Marie virginis in cancello Parochiali . . . . xxiiij s. iiij d.
De gilda sancti Thome Martyris in Cimiterio . . iij li. x s.
... gilda ex altare . . . . . . xxxvij s. vj d.
... gilda sancti Jacobi Apostoli ibidem . . . xx s. x d.
... gilda beate Marie Magdalene ibidem . . . xliiij s.
.... Sancti Georgii Martyris, viz. in Capella iij li. xviij s.
Summa xxiiij li. xvij s. vij d.

De gilda Corporis Xᶦ in ecclesia parochiali vj li. iij s. iiij d.
De gilda sancti Johannis Baptiste . . ix li. xiij s. iiij d.
De gilda de virginibus de fforstret Ais . . } v s. xj d.
De gilda de virginibus de Borestret . . }
De gilda sancti Petroci videlicet le Skynners & Glo-
uerys . . . . vj li.
De gilda sancti Dunstani et Eloy videlicet Smethis . vj li.

"fast and furious." In 1583 we find an order by the Mayor and masters of the
shocmakers "that at the ryding every master and journeyman shall give their
attendance to the stoward, and likewise bring him to the church upon pain of 12 d.
for every master, and 6 d. for every journeyman, for every such default, to the dis-
cretion of the masters of the occupation."

De gilda sancti Aniani Epi*scopi* viz. Corde-
nerys * . . . . iij li. vj s. viij d.
De gilda sancti Martini Epi*scopi* viz. Milwardys† liij s. iiij d.
Summa xxxiiij li. ij s. vij d.

De noua gilda apud le Bery de Ricardo Dakis et Joa-
chym Hoper . . . . xj s.
De gilda sancte Cruci*s* apud le Bery, vi*delicet* dc
Penses . . . . xvij s. j d.
De gilda sancte Anne apud seynt Nicholaum de Petro
Mason . . . . x s.
De arreragi*is* de gilda beate Margarete apud le Bore
de Thoma Bere . . . . . . vj s. viij d.
De gilda beate Marie de Walsyngam de Jenyn Sade-
ler et socio suo . . . . x s.
De gilda sancti Erasmi vid*elicet* de arreragi*is* de Jo-
hanne Cok, tanner . . . . . xiij s. iiij d.
De gilda sancte Anne apud le Bore de Johanne
Broker . . . . xx s.
De Johanne Hay de arreragi*is* de gilda apud le Bore iiij s.
De Johanne Renawdyn pro gilda sancti Dauyd apud
le Bore . . . . xj s. vij d.
Idem Johann*es* de gilda sancte Margaret*e* apud le
Bore . . . . iij s. xj d.
De gilda omni*um* sanctorum apud le Bore de Henrico
Moyle . . . . vij s.
De gilda sancti Dauyd in forestret de Adam Hicke . v s.
De gilda omni*um* sanctorum in Polestret de Thoma
Colom . . . . ix s.
De gilda sancti Cristofory apud le Bery cum Johanne
Philip xj s. sol*vit* v s. et res*po*ndet vj s.

* Bodmin has always been famous for its cordwainers or shoemakers.
† Millers are now sometimes called "Millards."

De gilda *sancti* Leonardi Ep*iscopi* cum *Ricardo* Dakys
& Rogenald Gwynnowe . . . . xxiij s. iiij d.

De gilda *sancti* Nich*olai* Ep*iscopi* at seint Nich*olas*
cum Ricar*do* Harry . . . . . iiij s. xj d.

De Gylda sancte Trinitat*is* apud Sanc*tum* Leonard*um*
cum ux*ore* Joh*annis* Bryant . . . . v s.

De gilda *sancti* Mathei Apo*stoli* apud le Bore cum
Joh*anne* Perryn, viij s. *manet per manus*, viij s.

De gilda *sancti* Martini Ep*iscopi* cum Joh*anne*
Bocher . . . . xxiij s.

Pleg*ium* Neell*ii* Lankelly & Joh*annis* Bryant & so-
lu*tum* . . . . x s.

De arrerag*io* gild*e* omn*ium* sanct*orum* apud le Bore
cum Joh*anne* Trelodrowe . . . . iij s.

De gilda *sancti* Cristofori apud le Bery A*nno* E[*d-
wardi*]. 9° rec*eptum* . . . . . xv s.

Summa

Mem*orandum* y recevyd for wex gaderyng of Church
this hier A*nno*.

ffrust *De* Will*ielmo* Androwe p*ro* Cera gild*e* sanc*ti*
Dauyd apud le forstret . . . . . ij s. vj d.

De sera sanc*ti* Lug Ewangelist de Tho*ma* Colom &
Joh*anne* Lyde . . . . . . x s.

De sera sanc*ti* Mich*aelis* de Joh*anne* Cok et Joh*anne*
Hancok . . . . xv d.

De sera sanc*te* Trinitat*is* de Ricar*do* Harry

De sera sanc*ti* Leodegarii de Gy Sadelere . . iij s.

De sera sanc*te* Clar*e* de Henr*ico* Sturtgyn . . iij s. iiij d.

De sera sanc*ti* Gr*e*gorii Pape de Petro Sadelere . xviij d.

De sera sanc*ti* Thome de Will*ielmo* Carpent*er* & Johanne Togyn . . . . xvj d.

De sera Beate Marie Virginis in le Porch in eccl*esia*
Parochi*ali* . . . . n*il*

De cera sanc*te* Trinitat*is* de Andrea Opy et Johanne
    Trelodrowe .   .   .   .   v s.
De cera sanc*te* Katerine V*irginis* de Johanne Don-
    worthy .   .   .   .   iij s.
De cera sanc*te* Kat*erine* de Thoma Wylliam .   .   iij s.
            Su*mm*a

Memorandum De rece*ptis* post festum sancti Michaelis
    Anno Domini 1470°.
Rece*pi* de no*ua* condonac*ione* circa villam.
De cera sanc*te* Kat*erine* .   .   .   .   .   . iiij s. xj ob.
De gilda sanc*ti* Aniani E*piscopi*   .   .   . xxvj s. viij d.
De limine sanc*ti* Stephani   .   .   .   .   . iiij s. v d.
De gilda sanc*ti* Martini E*piscopi*   .   .   .   .   x s.
De frat*ernitate* Marie Magdal*ene*   .   .   . vj s .viij d. ob.
De co*n*gregat*ione* sancte Clare   .   .   .   .
De frat*ernitate* sanc*ti* Jacobi .   .   .   .   . vj s. viij d.
De frat*ernitate* sancte Cruc*is* .   .   .   .   . vj s. viij d.
De frat*ernitate* Beate Marie in Cancello .   .   . vj s. viij d.
De frat*ernitate* Beate Marie in Capella sanc*ti* Georgii   vj s. viij d.
            Su*mm*a v li. xiij s. iiij d.

Also y yeff yn the town voluntarie as the paper makith.
    mensyon   .   .   .   .   .   . 1 li. viij s. j d.
            Su*mm*a 1 li. viij s. j d.

.   .   .   . recevyd for the bequest of Raf Dyer   vj li. xiij s. iiij d.
            Su*mm*a vj li. xiij·s. iiij d.

Memorandum that y haue recevyd off the Ildis of the
    town wich is graunted thorght the town .   .   .   .
    of the pore comenys ob*olus* a man.
ffrust of seynt Loye is Ihde off Thomas Colom   iij li. xvj s. v d.
Cum factura ij. wyndowys   .   .   .   . xlij s. .   .   .   .

Item of seynt Petrok is Ilde of Richard Dyuer . . xlj s.
Item of seynt John is Ilde of John Trevarthian et
   sociis . . . . vj li. xj s. ix d.
Item of seynt Anyan is Ilde of Thomas Wylliam viij li. xiij s. iiij d.
Et per manus Johannis Cok . . . . .
Item of seynt Martyn is Ilde of John Rawe &
   . . . for . . . . l s.
Item of the that be yn no Ilde of the Maier . . vij s. ij d.
       Summa

Also y haue recevyd dyuers other reseitis as hit
   aperith
ffrust of Thomas Lucombe for tymber y sold haishis *
   yn the licherise sold . . . . . v s.
Item of Joachym Hoper for tymber ther . . . v s.
Item of John Bere for xxx. there sold . . . vj s. viij d.
Item to the newe smyth for tymber sold . . . xiiij d.
       Summa

Item y recevyd of William Cok is wif . . . v s.
Item of John White for Henry Olyuer yef to the work viij s.
Item Henry Sturgen yef . . . . . . ij d.
Item the sone of Thomas Bodynyell . . . xl d.
Item of John Symon of Bod . . . . . . v s.
Item de Roberto Sperk Capellano . . . . iiij d.
De Davyd Witfen . . . . j d.
Item of Stephen Greby of the gaderyng of the Trinite †
   li3th . . . . iij s. iiij d. ob.
Item of Auery Skeis and Thomas Jerman . . ij d.
Item of Ciceli Serle for a crokke sold . . . xx d

* Ash-trees in the Church-yard.
† Money collected for Trinity lights or candles.

Item of John Hardy, Carpenter . . . xx d.
Item for a goys * y yeff . . . . . . ij d.
Item y recevyd a pipe of lyme y yef with Thomas
    lymby . . . .
Item y recevyd for a lome † y yef . . . . v d.
Item a nother lome . . . . . . iiij d.
Item per limine sancti Michaelis Anno regni regis Ed-
    wardi iiij^{ti} xj° . . . .
           Summa

Item of the maidenys yn fforstret . . . . vj s.
Item of seynt Thomas Ilde yn Church hay . . x s.
Item of the maidenys of the borestret . . . xvij d.
Item of John Rogger of Lonke y recevyd yn parti of
    payment . . . . vj s. viij d.
Item of John Davy, Draper, for a jorney . . . iiij d.
Item of a seruant of Thomas Jerman . . . iij d.
Item of the parish pepell . . . . xix s.
Item xviij s. per vicarium. Item de John Glyn v s.
          Summa iij li. xx d.

Also y recevyd of Corpus Christi is hilde of William
    Bodynyell and William Glyn . . . . iiij li.
      for the arrerages of Anno Edwardi iiij^{ti} x^{mo}.
Item of the Rydyng Ilde, viz. of Seynt loy is Ilde
    Anno Edwardi iiij^{ti} xj^{mo} . . . . . x s.
Item of seynt Petrok is Ilde . . xiij s. iiij d.
Item of seynt John is Ilde . . . . xxvj s. viij d.
Item of seynt Anyan is Ilde . . . . . x s.
Item of seynt Martyn is Ilde, iij s. iiij d. Anno Ed-
    wardi iiij^{ti} xj° . . . . . .

       * goose.   † lamb.

Item of the wardenys of the Parish Church, of Dauyd
    Witfen and Martyn Hogge, with Bere is part   xxxix s. ix d.
        Summa ix li. iij s. j d.

Item of the player * yn the Church Hay William
    Mason and his fellowis . . . . .   v s.
Item of John Skewis for a jornay .   .   .   iij d.
Item de William Perish for a rayelle   .   .   viij d.

This is the expens and costes don a pon the church of
    Bodmyn yn Byllynge of the . . . . . . hit a perith
    after.

ffrust for crecis . . . .   v d.
Item to William Mayowe for stonys to the grase ta-
    belle † . . . . ix d.
Item for . . . . . same stonys .   .   . xx d.
Item to Thomas Bodinyell for stonys for the same
    Work . . . . ij s. ij d.
. . . . . . ij. Berwys . . . .   iij d.
Item for a casier ‡ . .   . . . ij d.

---

* Fairs, markets, games, &c., were held in church-yards in early times, generally on the north side of the church. In the statutes, 13 Edw. I., stat. ii. c. 6, "the King commandeth and forbiddeth that from henceforth neither fairs nor markets be kept in Church yards for the honour of the Church." Plays and games seem to have lasted much later, for we find in the Visitation Articles of the Archdeacon of Suffolk in 1638, "Have any playes, feasts, banquets, suppers, church-ales, drinkings, temporal courts or leets, lay juries, musters, exercise of dauncing, stoole ball, foot ball, or the like, or any other profane usage been suffered to be kept in your Church, Chappel, or Church yard?"

† The grase tabelle is perhaps the plinth or course of stones immediately above the surface of the ground, or may be the string-course below the battlements.

‡ A sieve.

Item for parchementes for to make rollys . . .	j d.
Item for ly	
Item for grase tabelle stonys for seint John is Ilde .	iij s. vj d.
Item for fetchyng home f . . . . Organys . .	xv s. x d.
Item to William Perisch, Mason, for ij. jornayes vnder the grase tabelle . . . . . . William Dole for ix.	
jornayes at quarell	iij s.
Item to Thomas Gylle and his man a jornay . . . . . the grase tabelle	ix d.
Item ij. Quarteris dimid. of lyme . . .	iij s. j d. ob.
Item for viij. hurdelles to case	xiiij d.
Item to Thomas Opy, mason, j. jornay . . .	v d.
Item for stonys fo the chanseler dor and dr	ix d.
Item for ij. jornays to Ric. Richowe fo scapelyng * stonys for the grase tabelle	xij d.
. . . . . William Perish ij. jornayes & dimid . .	xij d. ob.
Item to Thomas Gylle for ij. jornayes under the grase tabelle	x d.
Item his man ij. journayes	viij d.
Item to Ude Hancok for v. jornayes to the same .	xxij d.
Item to John Hancok worchyng under the grase tabell x. jornayes	iiij s.
Item to Richard fforthe for xiiij. jornayes and dimid. apon the jambys of the chanseler dor and vpon the grase tabell yn seynt John is Ilde . .	vij s. iij d.
Item to William Mason for iv. jornayes, & dimid. to the same work	
Item to his man a jornay to the same . . .	
Summa	

Item for scapelyng of stonys to Pentewyn to John Hancok and his felowis	xj s.

* *Scapelyng*, rough-hewing.

Item for cariage of the same stonys from Pentewyn to
seynt Wynnowe . . . . . . xj s.

Summa xxij s.

Item to Richard Richowe for the taxk work,* that is to
seye, Receyvd for the pelerys yn iij. paymentes .

Summa xxij li.

Item the seide Richard hath Receyvd for the peloris
Betwene the chanseler and seynt John is Ilde yn
complete payment . . . . . . vj li.

Summa vj li.

Item delyuered to Richard Richowe and his felowys
for the taxke worke of the seide Wallys off the
South side, and on the Northe side . . . xij li
Item . . . . xx s.
Item die dominica ante festum Natalem Domini . x s.
Item ij° die Februarii . . . . . . x s.
Item . . . . iij li. viij s.

Summa xvij li. viij s.

Item payed to the seide Richard Richowe for scapelyng stonys at more for the wyndowys . . viij s.
Item to the seide Richard for the chanseler dore and
the gabell windowe yn Seynt John is Ilde for
scapelyng . . . . xviij s. vj d.
Item to John Hancok for the same work . . . iij s. ix d.
Item to Richard Richowe and to his felowys for drawyng ston at mor and scapelyng for the peloris
betwene seynt John is Ilde and the chanseler xxxv s. v d.

Summa iij li. v s. viij d.

* Contract for the pillars.

Item to Ric*hard* Richowe and his felowys, for dyue*rs*
    jornayes don:

ffrust to Ric*hard* Richowe ij. jornayes and di*mid.*
    apon the jambys of the north dor . . . **xv** d.

Item to Robe*rt* Wette*r* and Petrok Gwelys ffor xlix.
    jornayes for the wy̆ndowe a bowe the vysé **xxiiij** s. **vj** d.

Item to Petrok Gwelys and his feleship for drawyng
    and scapelyng stonys at Pentewyn . . . **xxxv** s.

Item for lond leve * of the stonys . . . . **v** s. **vj** d.

Item for cariage of the stonys fro Trewardreith . **ij** s.

Item to the Wener*is* † . . . . . . **ij** d.

Item to Ric. Richowe for xiiij. jornayes apon the
    gabell wyndowe . . . . . . **vij** s.

Item to Robe*rt* Wettor viij. jornayes to the same . **iiij** s.

Item to Petrok Gwelys for xviij. jornayes and di*mid.*
    apon the same . . . . . . **ix** s. **iij** d.

Item to Willi*am* Hayn*e* for xiiij. jornayes and di*mid.* **vij** s. **iij** d.

Item to Willi*am* Bettowe for xviij. jornais & di*mid.*
    to the sam*e* . . . . **ix** s. **iij** d.

Item to Morly for xiiij. jornais for the same . . **vij** s.

Item to Thomas Hancok for ij. jornais vnder the
    grase tabell . . . . **x** d.

Item to John Hancok for xj. jornais and di*mid.* apon
    the wyndowys . . . . . . **v** s. **vj** d.

Item for candele*s* to the masenys a fore Cristmas . **x** d.

Item for londe leve at Pentewyn . . . . **viij** d.

Item to Thomas Hayn*e* for xix. jornais and di*mid.*
    apon the north side . . . .- . . . **ix** s. **x** d.

Item to Petrok Gwelys for xiiij. jornais and di*mid.* . **vij** s. **iiij** d.

Item to Willi*am* Bettowe for xix. jornais and di*mid.*
    for the sam. . . . . **ix** s. **viij** d.

Item to John Hancok for xiiij. jornais to the same . **vij** s. **ij** d.

Item to Thomas Hayn*e* for xiiij. jornais to the same . **vij** s.

---

* Permission to quarry stones.   † Waggoners.

Item for candelles for the same worke after cristmas .   ix d.
Item y payed for scapelyng of the chapitaries* betwene
    the chancery and seynt John is Ilde   . .   ix s.
           Summa viij li. ix s. viij d.
           Tot. fol. lvij li. x s. ij d.

Item for cariage of the same stonys to seynt Blasy   .   xx d.
Item byeng the same   . . . . . .
Item to William Hayne iij. jornayes a bowte jambys
    of the north wyndowe   . . . . .   xviij d.
Item to Betty for iiij. jornays apon the samé   . .   ij s.
Item to John Hancok for ij. jornays apon the same   .   xij d.
Item to John Hancok for shittyng † of the newe work
    and the olde   . . . .   v s. vj d.
Item to Richard Richowe and his felowys apon the
    wyndowys yn the north side a weke after .   .   viij s.
Item to Robert Wettor and Petrok Gvelys and the
    feliship for xliij. jornays and dimid. apon the
    north wyndowys and the half arch sittyng yn
    the north side .   . . .   xxj s. ix d.
Item to John Hancok for xiij. jornays apon the same
    and ouer the stypell ‡ dore   . . . .   vj s. vj d.
Item to Thomas Hancok for vij. jornayes apon the
    same and dimid. jornay   . . . . .   iij s. ix d.
Item to Vde Hancok for v. jornayes apon the same   .   xx d.
Item to John Hancok for x. jornays and dimid. apon
    goter stonys and bergis § of the punyon ‖   . .   v s. iij d.
Item to Thomas Hancok v. jornayes and dimid. apon
    goter stonys and bergis   . . . . .   ij s. iij ob.

---

* Chapitaries, capitals of the columns.
† "shet" = "shut" = "closed" (Halliwell); "schetyng," *Prompt. Parv.*
"closing," a closing up.
‡ This steeple was destroyed by lightning in 1699.
§ *Berge* or *Verge*,—the projecting slate or tile overhanging the gable of a building.
‖ *Punyon*, a gable.

Item to Whitford Mason in mense Julii An*n*o E[*d-wardi*] iiij^ti x° at more . . . . .   x s. vj d.

Item to John Hancok at more xviij. jornayes apon
the garotts pilors and wyndowys . . .   ix s.

Item to Ade a *ser*uant for the masenys xv. jornays at
quari . . . .   v s.

Item to Robert Wettor, Will*iam* Hayn, & Witford at
quary lij. jornays . . . . . .   xxvij s.

Item to same feliship Rob*ert* and his felowys at Church
a pon the garettis and north wyndowys and parte
ther of quary iiij. j. jornay . . . .   xl s. ix d.

Item to Thomas Archer for mendyng a wall plate and
mendyng the drey . . . . . .

Summa

Also y paied for lyme . . . . . .   xiiij d.

Item to Robert Ber*e* iij. jornayes at quary . .   ix d.

Item for hurdel * . . . .   vj d.

Item for lyme y fet † Will. Matthy . . . .   iiij s. j d.

Item to Thomas Archer for mendyng the dreyes .   ij d.

Item to Robert Bere a jornay at q*u*ary . . .   iij d.

Item to Andr*ew* Glyn and John Glyn for cariage of
the rest*eris* fro Lestithiell yn Wenys . .   xvij s.

Item to Cowlyng & Shypper for cariage of tymber
fro Rep*erna* Newton and Glyn . .   v s.

Item to the seide p*erso*nys for iiij. M*il.* stonys . .   xj s. iiij d.

Item to Robert Bere for . . . .

Item for makyng the crane and the boket . .   vij s. ix d.

Item di*mid.* quart*er* lyme . . . . .   6 d. ob.

Item yn expens yn Wyn*e* to Tregarthyn for leve for
to have stonys fro the q*u*ary . . .   j d. ob.

Item for naylys for to amende the dreyes . .   xij d.

---

* "hurdel" = "harle," hair or wool (Halliwell).   † *Fet*, fetched.

Item for hausyng * the tymber hous and keuery * him
yn the Church hay . . . . . . xij d.
Item for v. bordis for the Church dore . . . iiij s. ij d.
Item to Lobbe for caryage of a tre fro Glynn . . xij d.
Item for a hours to bere the masenys gere to . . . . . iij d.
Item for a forest bylle † y yef to Tregarthyn for licens
to have stonys for . . . . xiiij d.
Item fillyng of treis at Glyn . . . . . vj d.
Item for lyme . . . . xiiij d.
Item for a pipa to mende the dreyes . . . ix d.
Item to Henry Carpenter for mendyng the dreyes . vij d.
Item to John Nicolyne for makyng synternys ‡ of a
wyndowe . . . . vj d.
Item to Robert Bere for sparres and to Baby for the
hous . . . . iiij d.
Item to Alic. Pole for strawe for theeth the walls . iiij d.
Item lyme y fet Seynt Wynnowe . . . . xj s.
Item for a quarter strawe to the mayer . . . vj d.
Item for a quarter strawe of John Togyon . . vj d.
Summa

Item to John Hervy for scafelyng tymber . . ij s.
Item for iiij. barelles § lyme, iij s. iiij d. fro Padestow
Item for 1 quarter lyme & dimid. . . . . xxj d.
Item for a pole of Bras for the crane . . . x d.
Item to Thomas Hay for a rope to the crane . xl d.
Item for strawe to William Mason . . . .
Item to Leye the thoch the hous . . . . iiij d.
Item for squaryng the treis that Joh. Arundell,
knyght, and Joh. Hygow yef . . . . xx d.
Item for stonys . . . . vij d.

* Raising and covering. † forest bill, same as lond leve, above.
‡ Syntern or centre, a frame of wood to support an arch in huilding.
§ The cost of lime averaged 3d. per bushel, 1s. per barrel, 1s. 4d. per quarter
from 4s. to 4s. 5d. per pipe, and 12s. per last.

Item for cariag of lyme fro Pendevy . . .	x d.
Item to laurence Renaudyn for cariag ij. pipis of lyme fro Pendevy	xvj d.
Item y paiede for a last of lyme at Padestowe . .	xij s.
Item for iiij. Mill. latthis at Padestowe . . .	xxxvj s.
Item y paiede to Raf. Hopkyn for iij. Mill. .	xxv s.
Item for freit of the same latthis	viij s.
Item for beryng and caria the same latthis . .	ix d.
Item to John Lyde for worchyng apon the synteris .	vj s. iij ob.
Item for lyme	iiij s. ij d.
Item for a rope	ij d.
Item for possyng * the chanceler	ij s.
Item to John Wettor, Carpenter, for possyng the rof of the chancelor and mendyng the crane and other labor	viij s. ix d.
Item iiij. pair tresis	v d.
Item for lyme	v s. v d.
Item for iij. pipis lyme at Padestow . .	xiij s. iiij d.
Item to John Bare to bere a letter yn to Devonshire to the Carpenteris	vj d.
Item to William Southrey for tynnyng nayls for the chanceler dore	ix d.
Item to Weneshot † borde for the same dore and other borde to ynne parte	iij s. vij d.
Item for twiste and crokis for the same dore xxij lb. .	xxij d.
Item for nailis with v strok hedes	ij s.
Item for workmanship of the dore . . .	
Item for other nayle	
Item for cariage of lyme fro Padestow . .	xij d.

Summa xvij li. xvij s. ix d.

Item for ij. quarteris and dimid. of lyme .	ij s. x d.
Item j. mill stonys	ij s. viij d.

---

* Propping the roof of the chancel, which was not then restored. † wainscot.

Item for iij. cariage of lodis of tymber fro the Park
wode . . . . . . ij s. vj d.
Item for drynk for Wenerys . . . . . ij d.
Item to John Benyt of Padistowe for iiij. pipis lyme xvij s. viij d.
Item for cariage of scafelyng tymber to Laurence Renaudyn . . . . xij d.
Item yn lyme fet at Kylle yn Maii and Witsonday
weke . . . . xviij s. iiij d.
Item for cc yren for a wyndowe yn the north side . vij s.
Item to John Jogyn for yren work and sertayn for a
wyndowe yn seynt John is Ilde, and a barre for
the quary . . . . xix s.
Item for small barre for a wyndowe . . . . x d.
Item the gabele wyndowe the yren work weyth
ccccliiij li. of the wich Sir John Kyngdon yef
cccxxxviij lb. and so ther was borth cxvj lb. and
that cxvj lb. came with the workmanschip xxvj s. viij ob.
Item for nailis to the dreys and scafelyng tymber . v d.
Item to Thomas Colom for the yren work and yren
for the ij. wyndowys yn the south side benethe
seynt John is Ilde . . . . . . xlj s.
Item to Thomas Archer vj. jornays apon synteris . ij s.
Summa

Also y paiede to John Lyde and to Mathew Carpenter
for scynt John is Ilde tymber . . . .
Summa xx li. xiij s. iiij d.

Also y paiede to Sam. Carpenter for the taxkwork
yn the north syde . . . . . ix li. xviij
Summa ix li. xviij s.

Also y paiede to John Hopkyn for c and dimid. &
xx lb. lede for the goteris . . vj li. xiij s. iiij d.
Item for cariage of the same lede . . . ij s. ix d.

Item for DCCCxij lb. of lede fro the mynys   .   . l s. xj d.
Item for DC   lede fro seynt Iva Parish   .   . xxxix s. xj d.
Item for D   lede for the north partis   .   . xxxiij s. iiij d.
Item for carie the same   .   .   .   .   .   . ij s. vj d.
Item for iij. quateris lede to the plumer   .   .   . v s.
Item yn expens fecthyng lede .   .   .   .   . iij ob.
Item for castynge and settynge lede xlj c. .   .   . xlj s.
Item for sauder lvij.   .   .   .   .   . xiiij s. iij d.
                    Summa xvj li. iij s. iij d. ob.

Also y paiede to Thomas Hawyt for viij. jornayes
      hewying stonys   .   .   .   .   .   . iij s. iiij d.
Item y paiede for vj. Mill. helyng stones   .   .   . xvj s.
Item for vj. lodes of cariage fro the more pelor stonys   xij s.
Item to laurence Renawdyn and John Hervy ffor
      cariage fro Pentewyn ix. semys   .   .   . ij s. x d.
Item yn drynk to theym   .   .   .   .   . j d.
Item to Thomas Archer to mende the dreys   .   . ix d.
Item y paied for iij. pipis lyme   .   .   .   . xij s.
                    Summa xlvij s.

Also to William Carpenter of Bedyforth for parte of
      the taxk   .   .   .   . iij li.
Item for Angel   .   .   .   . vj s. viij d.
Item for bordis   .   .   .   . ix s.
Item at rader day * .   .   .   . xl s.
                    Summa v li. xv s. viij d.

Also y paiede to Robert Wettor and to his feliship at
      more for the iij. pelerouris & dimid. the Church
      dore, & porch dore, and wyndowys, and the
      makynge of seynt John is auter l. jornays .   . xxv s.
Item to Hayn, mason, xxv. jornays .   .   .   . xij. vj d.
Item to Whitford xlij. dayes for the same work   . xxj s.

                    * The riding day.

Item for cariage fro Pentewyn to Trewardreith . .	xj s. vij d.
Item y paied to Andre Opy for a pipe . . .	viij d.
Item to John Togyn for nayles for the knottis * and to stodel † and to the goter	xxij d.
Item to Thomas Colom for nayl to the same . .	iiij d.
Item paied to Ronold Mason for helyng yn the north syde	vj s. viij d.
Item to Thomas Gylle for helyng there . . .	vj s. viij d.
Item y paide to Amys Codan for stodel . . .	viij d.
Item to Thomas Gille and Ronold Mason for the sam work	v s.
Item to John Nicoll, Carpenter, for makyng the goter for the plumer	xv d.
Item to John Antony for the same	xv d.
Item a tre y borth of Jervys Tayler . . .	viij d.
Item for makyng of a Mill. pynnys	ij d.
Item for a hacth naylc	j d.
Item to Thomas Hawys for helyng yn the north Ilde	v s. viij d.
Item for lyme	ij s. viij d.
Item for iij. treis . . . . . . Devyok . . .	ix d.
Item for iiij. Mill. ston	x s. viij d.
Item to Ede Hancok for seruynt the helyng . .	vij s. viij d.
Item to John Anteny fore tymber fore the south goteris	xxij d.
Item for cariage of the north tymber . . .	ij s. viij d.
Item to Richard Trote to ride to gete carer for the newe tymber	x d.
Item to John Hogge for housyng latthis and lyme	xvj d.
Item to Petrok Gwelys xix. dayes at more .	ix s. vj d.

* *Knottis*, bosses.

† "stodel?" = stadell, a support. This, however, is very doubtful, for the explanation does not agree with the use of the same word four lines below. It is probably some ancient local term.

Item to John Oggere for iij. pip*is* lyme & a barell ij s.
for cariage . . . . . .

Item to John Helyere for iiij. M*ill.* pynnys . . viij d.

Item to John Renawdyn jun*er* for cariag tolys to the
more and too semy*s* * stonys home ayen . . viij d.

Item lather for p*ar*getyng † seynt John is Ildc . . viij d.

Item to John Austell for seruyng the Carpent*er* ij.
dayes . . . . viij d.

Item to Laurens renawdyn for scafelyng tymb*er* . viij d.

Item for vj. pair*es* glovys to the Carpent*er*is . . vj d.

Item for lyme to drew at seynt Wynnowe . xiij s. iiij d.

Item to Will*iam* Hamond for a cariag fro thc more ij s.

Item to Cowlyng*e* M*ill.* ston*es* . . . . . ij s. x d.

Item to Huet iiij. M*ill.* ston*is* . . . . . xj s. iiij d.

Item to Hewet for iij. cariag*is* fro the more . . v s. x d.

Su*mm*a lxx li. xv s. vij d.

Item for iij. M*ill.* ston . . . . viij s.

Item for a payuer ‡ . . . . iij d.

Item for a casier . . . . iij d.

Item payed to Gybbe for wynde berg*is* and the
cariag*e* is . . . . . . iiij s. vj d.

Item for grete stonys and tabell stonys . . . vij s.

Item to Ric*hard* ffree and his felowys for gret*e* stonys
and tabell stonys . . . . . xviij s.

Item for ij. M*ill.* ston*es* . . . . . v s. j d.

Item for cariag*e* fro the downe thc same tyme . . iiij s.

Item to Shipper*e* and Cowlyng for ij. M*ill.* stonys . v s. ij d.

Item ij. cariag*es* fro the more . . . . . xl d.

Item to Rog*er* Stevyn for a lett*er* beryng to Tavystok vj d.

Item to John Hygowe and Losquit for drynk bryngyng
to the Church a tre . . . . . . ij d.

Item j. bushel of lyme . . . . . . iij d.

* loads.   † Laths for plastering.   ‡ pavior.

Item to John Nicolyn and Antony for makyng of
too sengelere* yn Ilde of Corpus Christi and yn
the Chancelere . . . . . . xvj d.
Item to John Helyer for v. Mill. ston hewyng . . ij s. j d.
Item Henr. Panter for help wene tymber . . . iiij d.
Item for cariage of a tre y fet at Holewich Master
Avery yef . . . . xij d.
Item for iiij. Mill. stonys x s. & viij d. of Thomas
Berewek . . . . . .
Item to John Antony for worchyng apon the goteris xxij d.
Item for ij. Mill. stonys of Russell . . . v s. ij d.
Item for cariage fro seynt Stevyn the same time . xl d.
Item for ij. semys sond for the plomer . . . ij d.
Item to Russell and Huet for iij. Mill. stonys . . viij d.
Item for iij. lodis stonys fro the more the same tyme v s.
Item to John Nicoll Antony for sawyng and worch-
yng apon the goteris . . . . . iiij s. vij d.
Item to Thomas Heuet for ij. Mill. stonys . . v s. iiij d.
Item to Thomas Russell for a lode of stonys fro the
more . . . . xx d.
Item to Ric. Carpenter and to Thomas Reue for sawyng
and worchyng apon the goteris . . . ij s. viij d.
Summa v li. xj s. iiij d.

Also y paiede to the helyeris that helid † the Church:
ffrust to Thomas Gylle for xiiij. jornays & dimid. . vj s. ob.
Item to Ronold Mason xiij. days & dimid. . . v s. vij d.
Item to William Perish for x. dayes & dimid. . . iiij s. ij d.
Item to John Roby for ix. dayes . . . . iij s. ix d.
Item to Thomas Hancok for xiiij. dayes & dimid. vj s.
Item to John Deyowe for x. dayes . . . . iiij s. ij d.
Item to a seruant of Thomas Gylle xiij. dayes & dimid. v s. vij d.

* Wild boars; figures of wild boars for some ornament, perhaps armorial.
† Helid, covered or roofed.

Item to a seruant to Ronold Mason for xiiij. & dimid. vj s. ob.

Item to Thomas Hawys for xiiij. dayes & dimid. . vj s. ob.

Item to Thomas Gille for vj. Mill. pynnys . . ij s.

Item to Thomas hancok for v. Mill. pynnys . . xx d.

Item to John Deyowe for iij. jornays . . . xv d.

Summa liij s. iij d. ob.

Also y paiede to John Hancok for helyng seynt John
 is Ilde yn taxk . . . . . . xx s.

Summa xx s.

Also y borth latth nayle of Bartholemew Trote ix.
 Mill. . . . . ix s. iij d.

Item of John Plumer j. Mill. . . . xvij d.

Item of Bartholemew iij. Mill. . . . iij s.

Summa xiij s. viij d.

Latth Nayl yevyn with Auery Skeys of Hayshpor-
 tone * iiij. Mill. . . . . . .

John Trelodrowe ij. Mill ccc. . . .

Henry Trelodrowe xviij. c. . . . .

De John Bosowe ij. Mill . . . .

De John Smyth Mill . . . .

De John Bowyer Mill . . .

De John Huc iiij. Mill helyng stonys . . .

De Thomas Berc we hadd his hous for the Carpenteris.

Thomas Lucombe glasid the gabill wyndowe yn seynt
 John is Ilde.

Bartholemew Trote and Rofe Dyer made the wyndowe
 and glasid next to seynt John.

William Olyver of Bodynyell made the next wyndow
 to that and glasid hym.

* Ashburton.

Odo Robyn & Pasch Robyn glasyd the nexte wyndow
to yn scynt John is Ilde.

John Watte glasid the wyndow yn the south next to
seynt John is Ilde.

Auery Skeys of Haysportone * yef the yre work a yre
of the large wyndow yn the south parti the west
wyndowe there.

Summa ix li. xiij s. j ob.

+ 1471⁰.

This is the expenc don hoc Anno post festum Pasche.

ffrust for lyme to John Benyt of Padestowe v. pipis .	xx s.
Item to John Anteny for makyng iiij. synternys and ij. dreyes	xv d.
Item for hurdels	vij d.
Item for hurdels . . . . · .	xiiij d.
Item for nayls to mend the dreys	j d.
Item for cariage of vij. barells lyme fro Pendevy to Thomas Hendy and Laurence Renawdyn . .	
Item for cariage of xviij. barells to theym . .	ij s. viij d.
Item for a pipe of lyme to John Benyt . . .	iiij s. iiij d.
Item y paied to Richard Fre for stonys for . . . . . . tabell	vij s. j d.
Item to Will. Hamond for cariage fro the more	iij s. iiij d.
Item for a last of lyme at Padestowe . .	xij s.
Item for cariage of lyme . . .	ij s.
Item for cariage of neldis for scafelys . . .	vj d.
Item y paid for hokis to the Church dore and to the vyse dore xlviij lb. Summa	iiij s.
Item for hokis to bere the lede pipis . . .	vij d.
Item y paied to William Mayow for stonys for the gras tabell and goter stonys	vij s. j d.
Item to William Hamond for cariage fro the more	xx d.

* Ashburton.

Item y paied to Patrik Lynch for chengyng of a
    bad nobill wich was recevyd of seynt Martyn
    is Ilde . . . .   viij d.

Item to William Hamond for cariage fro the more . xxv s. v d.

Item to William Hamond for cariage of xiij. lodis fro
    Bodynyell . . . . iiij s. iiij d.

Item for xij. hurdel . . . . . . xxj d.

Item for a berewe . . . . ij d.

Item for a half pipe . . . . . . iiij d.

Item to the masonys for worchyng vnder the gras
    tabell afore Witsonday yn the South parti and
    the porch . . . . xxxiij s.

Item for a quarter lyme . . . . . xvj d.

Item Mill. stonys . . . . ij s. viij d.

Item to John Davy of Padystowe for xx. barell . xix s.

Item to John Tailer for cariage of stonys fro the . . .
    and lyme . . . . ix s. vj d.

Item for ij. barell of lyme to William Malet . . ij s.

Item . . . . . . ij. barell of lyme . . . . ij s.

Item y paied for iiij lb. lede for the hokis to the
    Ch . . . .

Item to William Hamond for a cariage fro the more xx d.

Item for vj. lodis fro Bodiniell . . . . ij s.

Item y paied to William Tregonwell and his broder
    for lyme . . . . xxij s.

Item for Raysn for the wyndowys . . . . ij d.

Item to John Androw carier yn drynke . . . ij d.

Item y paied to Thomas Bodynyell for stonys for the
    gras tabell . . . .
            Summa ix li. xiiij s. x d.

Also y payde to Thomas Colom for ij. wyndowys yre
    work cccclxix lb. . . . . . . xliij s. j d.

Item to John Togyon for a wyndowe . xxj s. viij d.

Item for drynke to theym . . .   ij d.

Item for strawe for keueryng of the south wall and
the Porch dimid. c and dimid. quarter . .   xij d. ob.

Summa

. . . . . . y haue paied to Sam. Carpenter for parti
of the taxk of the rof yn the South Ilde Anno
E. iiij^{ti} xi^{mo} as hit aperith by a count betwene
the seide Sam and me . . .   vj li. xvj s. viij d.

   Summa vj li. xvj s. viij d.

. . . . . . y haue paied to Richard Richow and to
Robert Wettor ffor the taxk work, pelouris,
porch, and wall yn the South parti hath recevyd
xiij li. xj s. viij d.

   Summa xiij li. xj s. viij d.

Also y paied to John Donworthi for cariage of lyme   xiiij d.

Item lathis y caried fro Pendevy . . . .   iiij d.

Item for ij. lodis fro the more with hors and caria the
masons tolis . . . .   x d.

Item to William mason is broder for makyng the
stondyng vnder seynt Johns fote and the other
syde . . . .   xl d.

Item the masonys at More yn Laynte Anno Edwardi
4^{ti} xij^{mo}.

Ric. Richowe xxj. days . . . .   x s. vj d.

Item Robert Wettor xxvij. jornays . .   xiij s. vj d.

Item Richard Witforth xxvj. days . . .   xiij s.

Item William Hayn xxvj. days . . .   xiij s.

Item y paycde for stonys caried fro Pentewyn to
Trewardreith . . . .   iiij s. vij d.

Item ij. workmen hirid at more j. day . . .   viij d.

Item John Tayler for cariage of his carte at More .

Item for naylis for the Middell Rof . . . .   viij d.

Item for expenc to Richard Trote for to labore to
have the tymber home . . . .   x d.

Item for naylis for the goteris and the Middell Rof .   iij s. iij ob.

Item for cariage of free stonys fro Pentewyn ad Trewardreith . . . .   x s.

           Summa

Also y paied to John Hancok for parti of the taxk
x s. wich the masonys axith xl s. with the seide
x s. of the ffrust taxk of the peloris.

Item pro quarter lyme Johanni White .   xvj d.

           Owne a countid.

After this y payed to William Malet over that John
Bryant yef to the work ij s. for lathis, that is to
sey, Mill. wich seruyd this last work.

Item to Richard Bryant for crestis . . .   xxij d.

Item to Thomas Margaret for lath nayl . .   viij d.

           Summa xxxviij li. xxiij d.

Ultimo anno E. iiij^{ti} xij°.

Compotus Thome Lucombe maioris pro ffabrice Ecclesie a die Sancti ffrancissi usque mensis Junii
Anno Edwardi 4^{ti} 12°.

Inprimis receptum de parochia ex vetere debito pro
medietate anni, viz. tempore Thome Jerman .   xxxv s.

Et receptum tempore Thome Jerman de j. die Septembris xxv s. iij d. de diuersis parcellis, viz. de
Ricardo Tayler, de Thoma Rechyn et aliis .

Et recepi pro isto Anno de j. die Septembris   iij li.

Et de congregatione Sancti Luce Euangelist .   ix s.

De uxore Joh*a*nnis Jagow iiij s. ij d. tempo*re* Jerman

Et de *beate* Marie in Cancellar*io*	ix s.
Et Benedict Traer . . . . . iij li.	vij s. viij d.
Et de l*i*mine Sancte Kạterine	v s. vij d.
Et de l*i*mine Sanc*ti* Stephani	viij s. j d.
De diu*ersis* hom*i*nibus in penijs dat*um* . . .	iiij s. ij d.
Et recepi in Eve Pasche ap*u*d le Bery *pro* fabrice Capell*e* ibidem	iij s.
Et pro j. plank vendit*o* in eccl*e*sia	iiij d.
De gild sanc*ti* Georgii . . . . ' .	xxx s. j d.
Et de donat*ione* mulier*um* congre*gationis* in Eve Pasche	xxij s. iij d.
Et de gil*da* Corpo*ris* Chri*sti* . . .	v li. vj s. viij d.
Et de gil*da* Erasmi . . .	iiij li. ij s. vij d.
De l*i*mine leodegari	xv d. ob.
De gil*da* sanc*ti* Jacobi	v s. vj d.
De Maria Magdạlena	xiij s. v d.
De l*i*mine Gregorii . . .	xxiij d.
De sancte Clare	iij s. vij d.

S*umma* xxiiij li. xvij s. vj d.

M*emor*and*um* de expenc*is* *pro* ffabrica Ecclesie.
Inp*r*imis sol*utum* Joh*a*nni Sạm Carpent*er* in p*ar*te

sol*u*t*i*onis	xiiij li.
It*em pro* creci*s*	xvj d.
It*em pro* cariag*e* de le more ij. cariag*is* . . .	viij d.
Et pro cariag*e* de Lyme de Pendevy . . .	ij d.
It*em* Ric*ardo* Wetter c*um* sociis suis *pro* scapelyng ad More	viij s.
It*em* seruient*i* ib*i*d*em* 4 dies	xvj d.
It*em* j. qu*ar*ter lyme	xvj d.
It*em* Ric*ardo* Wetter *pro* le Taske et Ric . . . . . . vij li. viij s. In parte solucionis et iij li. . .	
It*em pro* cariag*e* de la carte ab More usq*ue* Trewar-dreith	x d.

Item licencia pro terra apud le More	x d.
Item pro le keueryng pro le wall	iiij d.
Item xij. barell lyme	xij s.
Item pro cariage	iiij d.
Item Waltero fforth pro keuere le porch	vj d.
Item workmanship tymber pro le porch	ix s. j d.
Item j. pipe lyme	iiij s.
Item ij. quarteris lyme	ij s. viij d.
Item for raggis for le porch	v s.
Item Wetter xiij. jornayes pro le porch	vj s. vj d.
Item Hayne xvij. jornays	viij s. vj d.
Item Whitefford xvj. jornayes	viij s.
Thomas Hancok xiiij. jornayes	v s. x d.
Ric. Richow v. jornays	ij s. vj d.
Item for grete Raggis for the Porch	xiij s. x d. ob.
Item William Hamelyn ix. lodis for axse	xv s.
Item ad Walter Bocher for carpenter work	
Item for lede & cartyng	v s. iij d.
Item for ij c. lede	xiiij s.
Item for iiij. barells lyme	iiij s.

Proximo Anno.

Memorandum de compoto Thome Lucombe et Thome
Jerman receptorum pro fabrica ecclesie Bodminie
A . . . . . .
Inprimis receptum de proficuis Ecclesie condonatis
per vicarium pro Vno anno integro xxvij li. viij
. . . . inde ad presbitrum ad seruiendum
curiam *   .   .   .   .   vj li. xiij s. iiij d.
Et sunt de claro recepta .   .   .   .   . xx li. xv s. v d.
Summa xx li. xv s. v d.

* The Vicar appears to have given a year's income, 27l. 8s. 9d., deducting from it
the Curate's salary, 6l. 13s. 4d.

Item *receptum* de gilda equit*um* f   *pro* cor*um*
Jantacle * condonat*um* per *communitatem pro*
eodem A*nno* et A*nno proxime* sequent*i* . ix li. vj s. viij d.
          S*umma* ix li. vj s. viij d.

Item *receptum* de gilda sanc*ti* Tho*me* Mart*yris* in
    cimit*erio* . . . . xl s.
Et de Joha*nn*e Yeme cl*er*ico *pro* ux . . . . . ffull*er*
    de Plymmouth . . . . . xxvj s. viij d.
Et Tho*mas* Lucomb dedit . . . vj li. xiij s. iiij d.
          S*umma* x li.

M*emorandum* qu*od* sol*utum* *pro* tymb*er* empt*o* yn
    diu*ersis* loc*is* . . . . . vj li. xix s. viij d.
Item *pro* scapelyng . . . . . . xiij s. x d.
Et *pro* cariage . . . . vij li. viij s. x d.
Item 4 M*ill.* stonys . . . . . . xij s.
Et factura le workhous . . . . . xxij s. xj d. ob.
Et *pro* fac*t*ura dreys et berwys . . . . ix s. x d.
Item *pro* groundyng the Wallys . . . . liiij s. xj d.
Et Will*iel*mo Carpent*er* de Bedy*f*orth *pro* part*e* of the
    taxk . . . . xv li. viij s.
Et plum*er* *pro* campanib*us* . . . . . xix s. viij d.
Et Joha*nn*i Rogg*er* de lonk . . xliiij s. viij d.
Et Will*iel*mo Hop*er* . . . .

---

* See note, page 4. *Jantacle*, another name for the Ridyng and sports;-from
j aunt.

A*nn*o E[*dwardi*] iiij^{ti} ix° x° et xj° usq*ue* fe*stu*m sanc*ti* Mich*ae*lis Arch*a*ngeli.

Comp*otus* of Thomas Jerman recever of the byllynge of the Parish Church of Bodmyn.

In*pr*imis recevyd for old tymb*er* and too wyndowys
sold . . . . iiij li. xx d.
Su*mm*a iiij li. xx d.

Also for wexe p*er*teynyng to the church, and other mony recevyd as the pap*er* apere*t*h . . iiij li. xviij s.
Su*mm*a iiij li. xviij s.

Als*o* of dyu*er*s mony of strang*er*is and of arrerag*es* and old ger*e* sold as hit aperith . iiij li. xij s. viij d.
Su*mm*a iiij li. xij s. viij d.

Also recevyd of the v. stewardis A*nn*o Edwardi iiij^{ti} by a composiscon for ther dyu*er*ys as hit aperith yn the paper . . . iiij li. xiij s. iiij d.
Su*mm*a iiij li. xiij s. iiij d.

Also he hath recevyd of the Ildis p*er*tynynge to the Church and Parish*e* as hit aperith by his pap*er* lxix li. iiij d.
Su*mm*a lxix li. iiij d.

Also recevyd of gaderyng of Wexe silver as hit aperith afore . . . . . . xxxiij s. xj d.
Su*mm*a xxxiij s. xj d.

Also another of gaderyng of wexe and of *ser*tayn Ildis as hit aperith . . . . . iij li. xix s. v d.
Su*mm*a iij li. xix s. v d.

Also y recevyd of a graunt y yef voluntari*e* thorgh-*out* the town as hit aperith by th*e* namys . l li. viij s. j d.
Su*mm*a l li. viij s. j d.

Also y recevyd of the bequest of Raf Dyer   vj li. xiij s. iiij d.
Summa vj li. xiij s. iiij d.

Also y recevyd of a grant ygreid thorghout the town
j d. a weke of a man, and obolus of serteyn personys delyuered by sertayn receuerys as the paper
aperith . . . .
Summa xxiiij li. xiij s.

Also y recevyd for Ayshis sold yn the Church hay . xvij s. x d.
Item alia parua . . . . . xxix s. viij d. ob.
Summa xlvij s. vj d. ob.

Also of dyuers personys as hit aperith yn paper and
of the maydenys of the town Anno .   xxix s. viij d. ob.
Summa v li. viij s. iiij d. ob.

Also of Corpus Christi is Ilde A° E. iiij^{ti} x^{mo} and of
the ridyng Ildis A° Edwardi iiij^{ti} xj^{mo} as hit
aperith, and of the arrerages of the Wardenys
parcell therof . . . . ix li. iij s. j d.
Summa ix li. iij s. j d.

Summa totalis ix $\overset{xx}{}$ xvj li. vij s. iiij ob.   Respondeo
vij s. vj d. pro gilda of the wich reseit y payed
apon the bylling of the Church as hit aperith
yn this seide paper by parcell as hit was
paied . . . . . ix $\overset{xx}{}$ xiiij li. iij s. vj d. ob.
Et sunt debita de claro . . . . xxxvj s. iij d. ob.
Also y am chargit of vj li. xiij s. iiij d. of Thomas
Lucombe yn the l li. viij s. j d. and hit was
paied yn the sead acompot as hit aperit. Et
debet . . . . v li. iij s. xj d. ob.

Memorandum die veneris ante festum Simonis & Jude
Anno E. iiij^{ti}xj° Pro gilda sancti Eloy condo-
natum Anno Edwardi iiij^{ti}x^{mo} Thomas Colom
debet ex donatione et congregatione j d. per septimatim et obolum per compotum vj li. v s. iij d.
inde solutum in argento . . . . xxxiij s. iiij d.
Also yn makyng of to wyndowys xliij s. j d. Et
debet . . . . . . xlviij s. x d.

Gilda Sancti Aniani Episcopi debet pro eadem materia
x li. xvj s. ' vj d. Et solutum per compotum in
argento ix li. xiij s. iiij d. Et debet xxiij s.
ij d. ob. inde Johannes Cok solvit iij s. v d.
Johanni Watte.

Gilda sancti Martini Episcopi debet per compotum
iij li. x s. viij d. inde solutum l s. Et debet de
claro xx s. viij d. Inde solutum maiori iiij s. Et
Johanni Watte ij s. viij d.

Gilda sancti Johannis Baptiste debet ix li. vij s. ix d.
inde solutum vj li. xj s. ix d. Et debet de claro
lvj s. inde solutum maiori et Jerman xx s.

Gilda sancti Petroci iiij li. ij s. xj d. inde solutum
xlj s. Et debet xlj s. xj d. inde solutum iiij s.
v d. maiori.

Isti qui non sunt in gildis de Bartholomeo Trote maiore
reeptum vij s. . . . . . in manibus Thome Jerman.

Memorandum de v s. pro Jo. Glyn in manu Laurencii
Renaudyn et solutum sicut dixit maior in diuersis
careagiis . . . . xx d.

Memorandum quod sunt in Rotulo Thome Jerman a
retro de gildis et de donatione exonerata Thome
predicti ut patet in Rotulo cum distr   .   .   vij li. ix s. vj d.
Et cum Henrico Moyle v s.   Et cum Elena Wodecok   ij s.
Et cum domino Willielmo presbitero ij s. viij d. pro
old tymber empto
Pro primo Anno pro gilda sancti Eloy.

Memorandum quod est in manibus Thome Colom ex
ˉcongregatione j d. et obolus septimatim die Domi-
nico ante festum purificationis Beate Marie Vir-
ginis Anno Edwardi iiij^{ti} xj°   .   .   .   xlviij s. x d.
Et cum Ricardo Dyuer pro congregatione gilda sancti
Petroci a retro   .   .   .   .   .   .   xlj s. xj d.
Et cum senescallo sancti Martini Episcopi a retro   xx s. viij d.
Et cum Ricardo Tailer pro Gilda sancti Johannis
Baptiste   .   .   .   .   lvj s.
Et cum Thoma Willyam et Johanne Cok pro gilda
sancti Aniani Episcopi   .   .   .   .   xxiij s. vj d. ob.
Et cum Maiore pro illis qui non sunt in gilda   .   .

Memorandum de crestis pro ecclesia et xxvj s. viij d.
pro legato uxoris Roberti ffuller et ij s. ex donatione uxoris Johannis N . . . .

Compotus Ricardi Tailer pro gilda Sancti Johannis
Baptiste pro eadem condonacione pro primo anno
Summa onerata.

De quibus solutum vij li. xj s. ix d. Thome Jerman.
Et xx s. Thome Lucombe.   Et est in manibus
Johannis Trefarthian adhuc.   Et est in diuersis
manibus a retro ut patet, videlicet cum Roberto
iiij d.   iij s. x d.
Cok, Johanne Davy, Johanne Trefarthian, Wil-

      ij d.   ij s. vj d.   xvj d.
l*ielmo* Hunne, Henr*ico* Pant*er*, Amicia Cothan,
      iiij d.   viij d.
Will*ielmo* Androwe Jun*ʳ*, Elizabet Strypa, Ri-
    ij d.
cardo Wilkok.

                Summa a retro.

Ricar*dus* Wilkok recepit v li. iij s. ob. Et sol*utum*
in *summa* supradicta. Et Johanne*s* Trefarthian
soci*us* ei*us* recepit iij li. xiiij s. Et sol*utum* in
summa predicta iij li. ix s. iij d. Et sol*utum*
Thome Lucombe xv d. Et debet iij s. v d.
ob.

Idem Ricar*dus* compot*um* pro eadem pro 2° Anno.
Et est in diu*ersis* man*ibus* vid*elicet* cum Bartholo-
       v s. vij d.   iij s. ix d   xij d.
meo Trote, Will*ielmo* Trote, Johanne Watte,
      ij d.   ij s. iiij d.   xij d.
Rober*to* Cok, Henr*ico* Moyle, Thomas Sour,
      iiij d.   ij s. ij d.
Will*ielmo* Hogge, Johanne Mayow, Johanne
iiij d.   x d.   xiij d.
Davy, drap*er*, Henr*ico* Chekke, Will*ielmo* Laury,
      v d.   xij d.
Johanne Laury, tailor, Rober*to* Browne, Nicho-
xiiij d.
lao White, Henr*ico* Panter, Patrik Lynch, Wil-
       xiiij d.   xiiij d.
l*ielmo* Androwe, Ricar*do* Teyler, Will*ielmo*
iiij d.   ij s. ij d.   xiij d.
Lynne, Henr*ico* Kennystowe, Dauyd Barn,
      x d.   viij d.
Thomas Hogge, Rober*to* Besta.

Compotus Johan*nis* Wever recep*toris* de gilda sanc*ti*
Johan*nis* Bapt*iste* pro 3° Anno   . Summa
on*erata*. De quib*us* sol*utum* Odoni Robyn
recep*tori* v li. Et Johanni Rawe.

                   Summa

Et sic debet . . . . . . quod est in diuersis manibus

xvj d.

videlicet. Et est in manibus Roberti Cok, Hen-

v s. xiij d.

rici Moyle, Johannis Walter, Thomas Bere,

xiij d. iij s. iij d.

Johannis Besta, Johannis Mayowc, Johannis

ij s. iiij d. iiij s. iiij d.

Raulyn, Johannis Davy, Edmund Beket, Rogeri

xij d. viij d. xviij d.

Wodecok, Willielmi Hogge, Ricardi Tayler,

xij d.

Johannis Hoig Junr, Johannis Netherton, Jer-

viij d. iiij s. iiij d.

vys Tayler, Johannis Laury, Henrici Panter,

vij d.

Margarete Amore, Johannis Trefarthian, Odonis

vij d. xj d. xij d.

Senyowe, Raf Credy, Willielmi Androw Junr,

vj d.

Ricardi Bere, Johannis Watte, Bartholomei

Trote.

Summa quod recepit ante festum purificationis Beate
Marie vj li. xij s. j d.

Summa non recepta l s. v d. Et ix s. viij d. pro B. T.
et Jo. Watte. Et xviij d. pro Ricardo Tayler.

Gilda Sancti Eloy.

Compotus Thome Colom receptoris de gilda sancti
Eloy Episcopi pro anno . . . . . .

De quibus solutum Thome Jerman in argento, xxxiij s.
iiij d.

Et solutum in faciendo ij. fenestras ad fabricam eccle-
siam videlicet pro factura ferri, xliij s.

Memorandum quod Thomas Colom debet ecclesie

sancti Augustini *per* compotum Anno Edwardi
iiij^{ti} xiiij° v s. vij d.

Summa

Et sic debe*t* a retro quod est in diu*ersis* manibus, viz.

iiij d.

ut pate*t* vid*e*licet in manibus Thome Cartor,

ij s. ij d.   Sol. ij s. ij d.   xiiij d.

Emote Davy, Joha*nnis* Gwelis, Johanna Pascow,

xij d.

Janyn Sadeler, Robe*rti* Baby, Will*ielmi* Perish,

ij d.

Robe*rti* Sadeler, Joha*nnis* A . . . . . . Plemyn,
Joha*nnis* Hancok, Joha*nnis* Broch, Roge*ri*
Smyth . . . . . .

Compot*us* Joha*nnis* Togyon vt sup*ra* p*ro* 2° Anno
su*mma* on*er*ata.

De quib*us* sol*utum* Odoni Robyn x s. Et p*ro* factura
ferr*i* p*ro* fenes*tra* p*ro* le porch xij s. iiij d. Et
p*ro* debit*o* in tempor*e* Bartholomei Trote et
Thome Jerman xx d. Et pro factura ferr*i* p*ro*
fenes*tra* Joha*nni* Watte viij d.

Summa xxx

Et est in ma*nibus* Thome Lucomb p*ro* Will*ielmo*
Mason ij s. Et p*ro* Joachym Hop*er* ij s. ij d.
Et p*ro* dutistman xvj d. Ite*m* p*ro* Thoma Barbor xvj d. Et p*ro* Ewan Goldsmyth ij s. ij d.
Et p*ro* Petro Sadler x d. Et p*ro* Joha*nne* Plemyn xiiij d. Et pro Tho*ma* Hawys xvj d. Et
p*ro* Joha*nna* Pascowe xij d.

Su*mma* xiij s. iiij d. quos Thomas Lucombe solv*it* in
compot*o* suo vt pat*et* in compo*to*.

Et alloca*t* sibi diu*ersis* hom*inibus* qui*bus* alloc*a*vit in
op*er*ib*us* suis . . . . . . Gwelis . . . . . . xj d.
Et Joha*nni* Antony xx d. Et Joha*nni* Nycolyn

ij s. ij d. Et Mathæo Carpenter ij s. ij d. . . . . .

Mason ij s. ij d. Et Johanni Hancok Junr

iiij s. iij d.

Summa xiiij s. iij d.

Summa recepta retornata et allocata in opere. Et

iij s. . . .d. pro diuersis naylis vt per bill.

Item d . . . habent de . . . videlicet Johannes Bosow

xiiij d. j. panne. Johannes Gunner xvj d. j. pot.

Summa

ij s. ij d.
Isti qui sunt a retro Thomas Carter, Emot Davy,

Sol. ij s. ij d.   xiiij d.
Johanna Gwelys, Johanna Pascow, Janyn

xij d.   vj d.   ij s.
Sadeler, Johannes Trelodrowe, Robertus Baby,

xx d.   ij s. ij d.
Johannes Hatter, Willielmus Perish, Robert

xvj d.   v d.
Sadeler, Johannes Austell Junr, Johannes

ij d.   x d.   xiij d.
Plemyn, Thomas Hancok, Johannes Bronch,

vj d.   ij s. vij d.
Roger Smyjth, Johannes Goldsmyjth.

Summa

Compotus Sampsonis Trefrozowe pro 3° Anno.

De quibus solutum Odoni Robyn receptori xxiiij s.

viij d.

Et solutum Johanni Rowe x s.

Summa

ij s. ij d.
Et est in manibus Johannis Hancok Ju^r, Johannis

iiij s. iiij d.   vij d.   iij s. iiij d.
Togyon, Johannis Brenton, Thomas Colom,

viij d.
Thomas Hawys, carpenter, ... Johannis

ij s. ij d.   ij s. ij d.
Auto . . . . Johannis Nicolyn, Rogeri . . . . .

        ij s. ij d.   xiiij d.
tymber, Willielmi Perish, Henrici Trelodrowe,

      ij s. ij d.   viij d.
Roberti Baby, Johannis Davy, Thome Colom,

    ij s. ij d.   iij s. ij d.
Emota Davy, ... Gwelys, Johanne . . . . .

         j s. ij d.   xxij d.
Et distr   de Reginaldo Mason j vlt. Petro Sadeler

        xij d.   xiiij d.
j. parcell, Thomas Gimes j. vlt. Johanne Bosow

j. parcell, Tho . . . . pl. Waltero Bocher,

    ij d.   ij s. ij d.   ij s. ij d.
. . . . Johanne Hatter, Joachym hoper

        ij s. ij d.
mortuus est, Johanne Hancok sen[r].

Compotus Johannis Tanner et Thomas Willyam pro
congregacionis condonacione j d. septimatim et
oboli septimatim provt patet in papiro taxacionis
primo Anno.

Summa onerata inde Johannes et Thomas solvunt
ix li. xix s. x d.

Et sic restat a retro in diuersis manibus vt patet.

Compotus Stephani Greby pro eadem condonacione
pro 2° Anno.

          Summa onerata.

De quibus solutum Thome Lucombe xxx s. Et
Odoni Robyn liij s. iiij d. Et iij li. vj s. viij d.
Et xxj s. vij d. Et ix s. iiij d. Et sic restat a
retro quod est in diuersis manibus vt patet vide-

               iiij d   iij d.
licet in manibus Roberti Rush, Johannis Hick,

      iiij d.   iiij d.
Johannis Hay sen[r], Johannis Hay Jun[r], Johannis Cristian Jun[r], Nicholai Tomma, Johannis

ij d. ij s. ij d. xvij d.
Tomma wek, Raf Hopkyn, Johannis Austell,
 ij s. ij d. xx d.
Johannis Raulyn, Roberti Salte, Willielmi
 xj d. iiij d. ' xxiij d.
Symon, Roberti Leya, Roberti John, Johannis
 xij d. xij d.
Laury, Johannis Harry, tanner, Thome Toker,
 xij d.
Johannis Davy clawter, Johannis Harvy, Regi-
 ij s. ij d.
naldi Trefrozow, Ricardi Carante, Stephani
 viij d. xxj d.
Watte, Luke Powna.

Et habent plegium pro Thoma Hay j. pan ij s. ij d.
 Et pro Willielmo Bremhisgrofe j. pot pro xij d.
 Et pro Thoma Dakis xxij d. distr cum Thoma
 . Jerman. Et pro Johanne Harry ij s. j d. distr
 j. pan cum maiore. Et pro Johanne Laury
 distr j. pot ij s.

Ipsi qui dedere voluntarie ad ffabricam Ecclesie Bodminie.

FORSTRET.

Thomas Archer	.	iij s. iiij d.
Gy Sadeler	. .	iij s. iiij d.
Magg. Barbor	. .	viij d.
Thomas Barbor	. .	xx d.
Johannes Boswyng	.	xij d.
Sossely Serle	.	iij s. iiij d.
Johannes Beste	. .	
Thomas Wat Sen^or	.	xx s.
Thomas Wat Jun^or	iij s.	iiij d.
Ricardus Amor	. .	viij d.
Johannes Burnard .	xiij s.	iiij d.
Nicholas Gurdeler .	.	ij d.
Johannes Spede	. .	xx d.
Thomas Marget	. .	v s.
Pers Sadeler .	. .	xx d.
Oto Senyowe	. .	xij d.
Johannes Langman		v d.
Willielmus Burnard	.	viij d.
Walterus Bocher ´.	vj s.	viij d.
Willielmus Pole	. .	xx d.
Jervis Teylder		xx d.
Jenet Osborn	.	xij d.
Willielmus Seniow	.	xx d.
Johannes seruus eius	.	viij d.
Pasch. Robyn	. .	xx s.
Serik .	. .	iiij d.
Johannes Cok merser	viij s.	iiij d.

Joachym Hoper		v s.
Johannes Jamis	. .	xx d.
Ricardus Hunt seruus N.		
Colyn	. . .	iiij d.
Johannes Lythfot .	.	xx d.
Ricardus Harry	. .	ij s.
Ronold servus ejus	.	xij d.
Johannes socius eius	.	viij d.
Willielmus Southay	iij s.	iiij d.
Uxor Tre[fare?]ll cor-		
diner	. . .	xij d.
Johannes Hicke	. vj s.	viij d.
Patrick Lynche	. iij s.	iiij d.
Petrus Greby	. .	xij d.
Thomas Hardy	. .	xx d.
Stephanus Riceman	iij s.	iiij d.
Petrok Gwels	iij s.	iiij d.
Harry Clowter	. vj s.	viij d.
Nicholas Colyn	. .	xvj d.
Adam Hicke	. vj s.	viij d.
Bertholomeus servus eius		xij d.
Nicholas Colyn seruus		
Hardy .	. .	iiij d.
Stephanus Greby .	vj s.	viij d.
Johannes Gatty	. .	xx d.
Johannes Lyde	. iij s.	iiij d.
Johannes Jagow	. .	viij d.*
Janyn Sadeler	. xiij s.	iiij d.
Thomas Wat cordyner	.	xx d.

* Erased with pen.

Harry Storgen	iij s. iiij d.
Willielmus Storgen	xx d.
Johannes Davy draper	x s.
Johannes Wille	ij s.
Margery Andrew	viij d.
Johannes Trevarthian	ij s.
Johannes Skewys	xij d.
Jankyn Teylder	x s.
Joachym Teylder	xx d.
Johannes Prowte	xiij s. iiij d.*
Summa istius xj li.	iij s. iiij d.

Henricus Kemelston	iij s. iiij d.
Willielmus Andrew	iij s. iiij d.
Johannes Gyll	iij s. iiij d.
Willielmus Tomma	ij s.
Johannes Netherton	iij s. iiij d.
Thomas Crypson	vj s. viij d.
Johannes Hervy	iij s. iiij d.
Raw Karedy	xx d.
Johannes Wat	
Thomas Wotton	iij s. iiij d.
Jenet Trystram	xij d.
Parnell Rede	xij d.
Uxor Netherton	viij d.
Uxor T. Edmond	iiij d.
Nicholas Howe	vj s. viij d.
Royn Pewterer	xij d.
Raw Hopkyn	iij s. iiij d.
Johannes Laurens	viij d.
Ricardus Dyver	ij s.
Thomas Gyrman	xl s.

Thomas Hancok	ij s.
Perkyn seruus T. Gyrman	iiij d.
Johannes Oppy	vj d.
Ricardus Richard	iiij d.
Betty Trote	xl s.
Willielmus Trote	iij s. iiij d.
Willielmus Toker	xij d.
Harry filius eius	viij d.
6 li. 16 s. 10 d.	

xvij li. viij s. vj d.

Jankyn Phylypp tanner	iij s. iiij d.
Roger Grygge	xx d.
Elinor Wodecok	ij s.
Thomas Hendre	vj d.
Uxor eius	ij d.
Willielmus Andrew Junᵒʳ	xij d.
Thomas Southwode	vj s. viij d.
Rogerus Ronold	xx d.
Johannes Wade	ij s.
Thomas Hay	iij s. iiij d.
Johannes Donge	viij d.
Mayowe Meyne	xx s.
Ricardus Dyver	ij s. iiij d.
Johannes Laury Teylder	xij d.
Ronoldus Mason	iij s. iiij d.
Harry Trelodrowe	xviij c. neyll.
Johannes Dertemouth	x s.
Johannes Martyn	iij s. iiij d.
Johannes Hancok Senᵒʳ	v s.

* Erased.

Jennet Hopkyn . .	iiij d.
Johannes Trevarthyon	
hoper . . iij s.	iiij d.
Willielmus Laury . .	xij d.
Johannes Renawdyn .	xij d.
Ricardus Dakys .	xx d.
Rogerus Pers . .	ij s.
Jenet Pers . . .	
Thomas Body . .	ij s.
Johannes Gervy . .	vj d.
Henricus Moyll . vj s.	viij d.

4 li. 7 s. 6 d.

Johannes Broker . .	xij d.
Alic Monke . . iij s.	iiij d.
Michael Cobbe . .	xij d.
Nicholas Wat cherman .	xx d.
Johannes Leye . .	xx d.
Thomas Bere . .	xx s.
Johannes Trelodrowe[ ]Mij.C neill	
Johannes Hay Sen^{or} .	iiij s.
Wat Peryn . . .	iiij d.
Johannes Hay Jun^{or} .	iiij s.
Rawe Renawdyn . .	vj d.
Stephanus Hervy . .	xij d.
Thomas Rothen . .	xx d.
Johannes Cristian Sen^{or} .	xij d.
Johannes Cristian Jun^{or} .	xvj d.
Ricardus Devck . .	viij d.
Johannes Luke . .	xx d.
Johannes Daunce . .	xij d.
Johannes Wille . vj s.	viij d.
Johannes Trethewe .	viij d.
Johannes Hervy cordyner	xij d.

Johannes Hancok ma-	
son . . iij s.	iiij d.
Michael Rothen . .	ij s.
Uxor Johannis Useryn .	xij d.
Johannes Beryn . .	
Johannes Hancok smyth	xx d.
Emot Davy . . .	v s.
Johannes Jagowe . ij s.	viij d.
Johannes Malet . iij s.	iiij d.
Johannes Redreyth .	xvj d.

Summa 3 li. 14 s. 9 d.

Uxor Johannis Ston .	xij d.
Johannes Plymyn . iij s.	iiij d.
Samson Trefresow . .	xij d.
Johannes Corun . .	ij s.
Willielmus Dreyn . .	xvj d.
Nicholas Tankard . .	x s.
Robertus Cok . .	xx s.
Davy Hay . . .	xvj d.
Johannes Branche .	xx d.
Harry Panter . iij s.	iiij d.
Johannes Bolcpyt . iij s.	iiij d.
Johannes Bremysgrove .	viij d.
Uxor eius . . .	
Nicholas Russh . .	xx d.
Willielmus Hicke . .	vj d.
Johannes Kestcll . .	x s.
Robertus Russh . vj s.	viij d.
Johannes Davy clouter .	viij d.
Johannes Bosow .	ij^{ml} neyll
Uxor eius . . .	
Jamis Tregustok . .	xij d.
Johannes Bony . .	xij d.

Luke Powne	.	iiij d.	Johannes Walter	.	ij s.
Johannes Cradok .	.	xij d.	Robertus Hoke	.	xij d.
Johannes Taberer .	.	viij d.	Willielmus Hoygge		xx d.
Johannes Bryand de fowy		iiij d.	Johannes Wat Junᵒʳ		ij s.
Harry Bosowe	iij s.	iiij d.	Willielmus Dole	.	xx d.
Johannes Tankard	.	xij d.	Johannes Wat Koc		xx d.
Johannes Skever .	.		Thomas Wener Junᵒʳ	.	xij d.
Thomas Body	.	xij d.	Uxor eius	. .	iiij d.
Summa 3 li. 7 s. 2 d.			Summa 3 li. 6 s. 6 d.		

Michael Luky	iij s.	iiij d.	Ricardus Trevarthyan	iij s.	iiij d.
Davy Toker .	iij s.	iiij d.	Ronoldus Bryand .	.	v s.
Willielmus Body	.	vij d.	Johannes Bryand .	vj s.	viij d.
Remfre Rothen	.	ij s.	Johannes Renaudyn myl-		
Jenet Syngwell	.	iiij d.	ler	. .	xx d.
Thomas Wyllyam .	xiij s.	iiij d.	Uxor eius	. .	vj d.
Johannes Benet	.	xij d.	Thomas ffycke	.	
Thomas Gwennow	.	xij d.	Jenet Bryand	.	xij d.
Oto Gwyn .	.	xv d.	Johannes Austell smyth		
Thomas Gyll	.	xx d.	Mˡ neyll	.	ij s.
Johannes Carpenter	.	xvj d.	Johannes seruus eius	.	xij d.
Thomas Webber Senᵒʳ	.	v s.	Johannes Kethe	.	iiij d.
Walterus Renawdyn		xij d.	Johannes Prey	.	xij d.
Johannes Salysbery	.	iiij d.	Johannes Davy laborer	.	
Johannes Hicke coryer	.	viij d.	Jenet Byebery	.	ij s.
Harry Checker	.	xij d.	Robyn Broun	.	iiij d.
Johannes Skoveryn	.	xij d.	Pascow Lokyer	.	ij s.
Rogerus Cornysh .	.	viij d.	Johannes Harnan .	.	j d.
Wyllielmus Broun		vj s.	Ricardus Hoygge .	.	viij d.
Ricardus Columb .		xx d.	Johannes Calway .	.	vj d.
Johannes Edmund	.	xij d.	Isabella Laury	.	iiij d.
Johannes Braunch Ser	.	viij d.	Annys Baby .	.	iiij d.
Martynus Beryn	vj s.	viij d.	Alic Hoygge	.	ij d.
Johannes Rodde	.	vj d.	Johannes Randowe	.	xij d.

Thomas Helman .	viij d.
Ede Hancok . .	xij d.
Annis Provys .	iiij d.
Johannes Trygge .	iiij d.

BAGGE LANE.

Ricardus Davver .		viij d.
Johannes Thomas Gorlek		vj d.
Robertus Salt .		xx d.
Nicholas Trethelyn	vj s.	viij d.
Baudyn Calway .	vj s.	viij d.
Item . . .		xij d.
Raubyn Blower .		iiij d.
Jenet Helston .		iiij d.

LOSTER STRET.

Johannes Paket smyth .		viij d.
Robertus Courtes .		vj d.
Martyn Nowell .		xx d.
Robertus Sadeler .	iij s.	iiij d.
Johannes Stephyn .		iiij d.
Luce Cote . .		xx d.
Ricardus Ber .	vj s.	viij d.
Johannes Russell .		
Johannes Bere .		xij d.
Kateryn . .		xij d.
Thomas Eme .		xij d.
Jenet Merefylde .		xx d.
Ricardus Fourthe .		
Perkyn Mason .		ij s.
Johannes Lokyer .		iiij d.
Rogerus Wat .		vj d.

Robertus Ley . .	xij d.
Jenet Kernek . .	ij d.
Johannes Anteney .	
Uxor eius . .	j d.
Cornelys Hoper .	viij d.
Thomas Robyn .	vj d.
Jenet Moyll . .	xv s.
Johannes Motty .	viij d.
Johannes Harry .	viij d.
Vryn Goldsmyth .	xx d.
Johannes Goldsmyth .	viij d.
Uxor eius . .	j d.
J. Trewcnyn .	xvj d.
Wyllelmus Teke .	viij d.
Item of the Mayer .	xij d.

HONY STRET.

Andrew Opy .		iiij d.
Richardus John .		xx d.
Ricardus Welet .	iij s.	iiij d.
Johannes Thoma .		xx d.
Thomas Columb .		xx d.
Robertus Baby .		viij d.
Johannes Botreax .		xij d.
Jenet Paschowe .	iij s.	iiij d.
Rawe Myllar .	iij s.	iiij d.
J. Raulyn tanner .		xij d.
Ricardus Senyowe .		xij d.
J. Thomas Wege .		xx d.
Johannes Penhale .		xij d.
Johannes Donworthy .		iiij d.
Johannes Courtes .		xx d.
Johannes Doune .		xij d.

Alicia Pole .	.	ij s. vj d.	Rector Hellondiæ .	xij d.
Willielmus Pole	.	. xij d.	Johannes Austell .	xx d.
Willielmus Koc	.	. xx d.	Uxor eius . .	xx d.
Thomas Guner	.	. viij d.	Johannes Togen .	xx d.
Johannes Raff	.	. xx d.	Johannes Brenton .	ij d.
Oto Robyn .	.	xx s.	Thomas Hawys .	xij d.
Florencia Wyte	.	viij d.	Johannes Derell .	xx d.
Margareta Swetman	.	j d.	Robertus Dole .	viij d.
Jenet Evyll .	.	. iiij d.	Ricardus Wyte .	xx d.
Jenet Teylder	.	xij d.	Mathy Carpynter .	xvj d.
Johannes Harry	.	. xvj d.	Robertus Laurens .	ij d.
Thomas Toker servus			Davy Baron . .	xx d.
Wyllelmus Mathy	.	viij d.	Ricardus Corant .	xij d.
Alicia Brystowe	.	. ij d.	Thomas Anwell .	xij d.
Pers Gascon .		iiij d.	Thomas Carter .	viij d.
			Uxor eius . . .	vj d.
CASTRET.			Johannes Raulyn .	vj s. viij d.
			Johannes Senyowe .	ij d.
Harry Wener	.	. xx d.	Johannes Royn . .	xij d.
Davy Witfen	.	. v s.	Johannes Gefferay .	iiij d.
Edmundus Beket .	xiij s.	iiij d.	Alicia Fletcher . .	j d.
Ricardus Bere	.	. xij d.	Margareta famula Res-	
Margareta Baby	.	.	karek . . .	iiij d.
Mathy Coke .	.	. xx d.	Ricardus Cleyth .	iiij d.
Jenet Gwels .	.	. viij d.	Alicia Tabbar .	xx d.
Jenet Tanner	.	xij d.	Waterus Bedman . .	xij d.
Ricardus Tholyn	.	. xij d.	Uxor Michaelis Helyer .	ij s.
Harry Sy .	.	. xx d.	Johannes Parke . .	xij d.
Seruus eius .	.	. iiij d.	Johannes Hicke . .	xij d.
Robertus Bere	.	. x d.	Jamis Codan .	xij d.
Pers Weuer .	.	. iiij d.	Johannes Munday .	viij d.
Willielmus Penvos	.	xvj d.	Uryn Scolemaster .	iij s. iiij d.
Wyllielmus Hune .	.	xij d.	Ricardus Nakys . .	
Alicia Bere .	.	iiij d.	Panston . .	viij d.

Nance Jagowe	iiij d.	Jenet Fowy .	.	.	iiij d.
Walterus Pyper	iiij d.	Johannes Dounyng	.	xij d.
Ebot Brasyer	iiij d.	Michael the mylar	.	xx d.
Ricardus Spicer .	j d.		

RYNE STRET.

Wyllielmus Pers .	ij s.

POLE STRET.

Mohun	
Thomas Olly . .	viij d.
Johannes Roby Coc .	xx d.
Willielmus Glyn . .	x s.
Johannes Coche . .	xij d.
Willielmus Carpynter .	ij s.
Uxor eius . . .	xij d.
Walterus Downe . .	ij s.
Ricardus Carpynter .	viij d.
Willielmus Mathy .	iij s. iiij d.
Johannes Rawlyn . .	xij d.
Robertus Dyer .	vj s. viij d.
Thomas Uryn . .	xij d.
Laurentius Roby . .	xij d.
Johannes Cok tanner .	x s.
Johannes Sporyer .	xij d.
Wyllielmus Symon	xx d.
Jenet Skenard .	xx s.
Thomas Skenard . .	viij d.
Thomas Trevelyn .	vj s. viij d.
Jenet Tanner . .	xvj d.
Harry Crypsyn . .	xx d.
Johannes Degendon .	xij d.
Jankyn Laury	xij d.
Robertus Ive . .	xvj d.
Johannes Harry .	iij s. iiij d.

Johannes Olly .	xij d.
Willielmus Pencors	
Johannes Hancok . .	xx d.
Johannes Robyn . .	xvj d.
Thomas Lucombe vj li. xiij s. iiij d.	
Nance Rescawrck . .	iiij d.
Stephanus Wat ' . .	viij d.
Johannes Helyer . .	
6 li. 19 s. 4 d.	
Thomas Robyn . .	xij d.
Johannes Fowy(?). .	iiij d.
Stephanus Sany solutum	j d.
Uxor Cambrygge . .	iiij d.
Johannes Anwell . .	
Thomas Hicke . .	iiij d.
Thomas Ruthen Junʳ .	xij d.
Uxor T. Wotton . .	j d.
Johannes Wyll servus	
Wytfen	vj d.
Emot Shypster . .	viij d.
Item of John Wat .	iij d.
Item Thomas Bonde .	j d.
Item for the beruall & the	
porpell garlemet *	vj d.
Ricardus Ronold .	j d.
Johannes Tregasow	j d.

* Probably a pall and trappings for burials.

CROCKEWYLLANE.

Robertus Beste .	xvj d.
Elyus Storgen . .	
Raf Stephyn . . .	viij d.
Margareta Hopkyn .	ij d.
Jenet Nycoll an anwell .	
Johannes Donnow	xij d.
Elizabetha Stryppe	iiij d.
Emot Tanner . .	viij d.
Wyllielmus Fremason xiij s. iiij d.	
Jamis Glover . iij s. iiij d.	
Item of a man of Walys .	iiij d.
Rogerus Walter . .	xx d.
Leonardus Gylys . .	viij d.
Thomas Bocher . .	xij d.
Isabella Reskarek . viij s. iiij d.	
Robertus Wener . .	viij d.
Nicoll famula T. Wat .	iiij d.
Johannes Cok Jun^or .	vj d.
Johannes Baron .	j d.
Thomas Witfen .	iiij d.
Harry Sebeley .	ij d.

Robertus John seruus Johannis Tankard .	iiij d.
Johannes Knygt servus Roberti Russh .	iiij d.
Johannes Bettow . .	xx d.
Wyllielmus Potter .	iiij d.
Henricus Ratynbry .	iiij d.
Annis Taber . . .	ij d.
Johannes Koc filius Willielmi Koc . .	iiij d.
Thomas Peuter Junr .	
Johannes Mayow servus Lucomb . .	ij d.
Johannes Huchyns servus Joachymi Hoper	iiij d.
Johannes Nicolyn . .	xiiij d.
Rogerus Yonge . .	xij d.
Harry Harry de Glyn .	x s.*
Ade Jun^or . . .	iiij d.
Sherston . . iij s. iiij d.	
[Math . .?] the leche .	xx d.
Morrys Tretheff . .	xij d.
Ricardus Peuter . .	iiij d.

* Erased.

www.ingramcontent.com/pod-product-compliance
Lightning Source LLC
Chambersburg PA
CBHW021637270326
41931CB00008B/1057